Contents

Say the Sounds	4
Tricky Words	5
Look Out For Me	6
Snakes	7
Deserts	25
Captain Scott	43
Underground	61
Mushrooms	79
Teeth	97
Book Review	116
Topic Review	118

This book belongs to

Say the Sounds

y
as in
silly

i_e
as in
kite

e_e
as in
these

o_e
as in
rose

u_e
as in
cube

a_e
as in
cake

Tricky Words
go
no
so
my
one
by
like
only
live
have
old
give
when
what
down
little
where
why
which
who

Look Out For Me

foxes

anaconda

Clement Markham

shark

deathcap toadstool

camel

Snakes

Snakes are reptiles. They have no arms or legs. There are about three thousand different sorts of snakes. Some snakes are very long and some are quite short.

A snake has scales to protect its skin from the hot sun. A snake's skin feels cool and smooth.

As a snake gets bigger, it has to shed its skin. The skin looks dull when it is about to be shed. The snake rubs its nose to loosen the old skin, which splits to let the snake slide out.

Snakes can glide on the ground and slide up trees. As a snake slithers along, the scales on the underside of its body grip onto the ground. Some snakes can swim too.

Snakes need the sun, but they cannot cool down by themselves. They have to hide from very hot sun. When it is cool, snakes are sluggish and sleepy.

Snakes normally hatch from eggs. The eggs have strong, leathery shells which do not crack if they are dropped.

A snake hides its eggs in holes in the ground or sand, or in gaps in rocks. A young snake is born with an egg tooth to help it get out of the egg when it hatches.

An adder has zigzag markings on its back. It is poisonous but the poison cannot kill you. An adder's eggs hatch inside its body so the young adders are born alive.

Some snakes spend the whole winter sleeping. They look for a hole to shelter inside, in the ground, or in a rock or a tree. They do not wake up again until spring comes.

Snakes are hunters. The bones in a snake's mouth are joined together quite loosely so they can spread wide apart to fit food in. The skin stretches around the food, too, as if it were made of elastic.

Rattlesnakes, or rattlers, live in North America. A rattler has a bit of dead scale at the tip of its tail. When it shakes its tail, the dead scale makes a buzzing, rattling sound.

Rattlers hunt small animals such as frogs, toads, and lizards. But rattlers are hunted themselves, too, by king snakes, opossums and roadrunners.

The biggest sorts of snakes are called constrictors. When it catches an animal, a constrictor coils its body around the animal and squeezes it hard.

The anaconda, which lives in South America, is the biggest snake of all. Anacondas can be more than 30 feet long.

Some snakes are poisonous and have poison, called venom. When a snake bites, it injects venom into its victim with its fangs.

The poison can be milked from the snakes. It can be used to make an antidote so that if a snake bites someone, they can be made better.

What's in the book?

What sort of
animals are snakes?

What do snakes usually hatch from?

What is venom?

What do you think?

Why do snakes shed their skin?

Are snakes dangerous?

Deserts

A desert is a big stretch of land which gets very little rain. Deserts can be made up of sand or of stones or rock. The Sahara Desert in North Africa is the biggest desert of all.

In some deserts, the sand gets piled up into mounds by the wind. These mounds, which look like waves, are called dunes.

Sometimes, strong winds whip the sand and dust up into sandstorms. When this happens, clouds of sand drift across the desert.

sandstorm

There are tribes who live in the desert. They use camels to ride on and to help them carry things. That is why camels are sometimes called the ships of the desert.

A camel stores fat in its hump. It can go without food or drink for a long time, while it uses up the store of fat. A camel can close its nostrils, which stops sand from getting up its nose in sandstorms.

Deserts often look empty, but lots of animals do live there. There is not much shade or shelter from the sun, so animals hide and do not come out until it is cooler.

Small animals, reptiles and insects shelter underground from the sun. Desert insects tend to have long legs which help them avoid touching the hot ground.

This insect is from the Namib Desert in South Africa. It drinks while standing on its head by kneeling down and letting droplets from the morning fog drip down its body and into its mouth.

This is a desert fox, called a fennec fox. It lives in the Sahara desert and hunts small animals and insects.

fennec fox

Roadrunners like this one live in deserts in America. They mainly get about by running along the ground, and they feed on insects, lizards and small snakes.

Deserts often go without rain for a very long time, but sometimes there are sudden rainstorms. When rain falls, the empty riverbeds fill up, and animals can come and drink.

When it has rained, the desert blooms, but only for a short time. Then the seeds lie waiting on the desert sands until the next rainstorm, when they can bloom again.

The cactus has adapted well to life in the desert. When rain falls and the soil is wet, the roots of the cactus take in as much rain as they can. The cactus swells up as it stores the liquid and then shrinks again, little by little, as it uses it up.

Lots of small animals and insects live on the cactus. Desert woodpeckers make holes for nests at the top.

Spadefoot toads live in deserts in America. They can spend a long time underground, waiting for rain. Then they come out into the pools of rain.

The tadpoles of the spadefoot toad only take three weeks to develop into adult toads. By this time, the pools have all dried up, so the toads go back underground to wait for it to rain again.

What's in the book?

What is the biggest desert?

What are dunes?

Where do some animals shelter from the sun?

What do you think?

Why are camels called ships of the desert?

Is the desert a difficult place to live?

Captain Scott

Antarctica is the continent at the southern end of the Earth. It is big and very cold, with tall mountains and deep holes. The South Pole is at the farthest south point of all.

It is very hard to get to the South Pole, and in 1900 (nineteen hundred) no one had been there yet. At that time, a man called Clement Markham was planning a trip to go to Antarctica. He chose a man called Robert Scott to head the trip. Scott was a sailor and a very determined person.

On the trip, Scott and the rest of the explorers came very close to the South Pole, but they did not quite get there. They made maps of the parts of Antarctica that they had explored. When they got home, Scott was made a captain and the trip became famous.

All the same, Captain Scott was not satisfied. He was determined to go back to Antarctica and to get to the South Pole. So this time, he planned a trip to the Antarctic himself. He tried to think of everything. He had biscuits made that did not freeze in the cold!

In 1910 (nineteen ten), Captain Scott sailed for the Antarctic again. His ship was loaded with all the things that he and his explorers needed. They took little white horses and husky dogs with them on deck and they had pet rabbits hopping around too!

But things soon started to go badly. The ship was hit by bad weather. Big waves crashed down on her. The animals were kept safely inside, but some of the men's things were lost and the ship ended up with a hole in her side. They had to stop and mend the ship before they continued.

Then Captain Scott got a telegram from a man called Roald Amundsen. It said that Amundsen was headed for the South Pole too. Scott was determined to get there before him, but it was going to be hard.

When he and his men got to Antarctica, they had to sail until they found somewhere safe to land and set up camp. Then it took them just under a week to bring all the stores and equipment from the ship to the shore.

They had one big tent and lots of small ones. They set up the small ones and lived in them until they had finished building a wooden hut inside the big one. Then they lived in the hut instead.

The Antarctic can only be explored in summer, as in winter the weather is too bad. Scott and his men did not arrive until the end of the summer. This meant they had to live in the camp for a whole winter and wait until next spring before setting out for the South Pole.

Before setting off properly, they went ahead and left piles of food and fuel along the trail. It was going to be hard to carry all the things they needed with them, so these piles were to help them if they ran out of food and fuel on the trek back from the Pole.

It was a long, hard trek to the South Pole. They had to bring tents to sleep in as well as food, drink and wood. The horses and dogs helped, but for much of the time the men had to drag everything themselves.

Only four men were picked to go with Scott to the Pole itself. The weather was terrible so the trip took longer than they had planned. When they got to the South Pole, they found a flag and a letter left by Amundsen, who had been there several weeks before. Scott was very disappointed.

The trek back was very, very hard and it did not go well. One man fell, hit his head and died. The rest struggled sadly on. Then one of them, a man called Captain Oates, got very bad frostbite and had difficulty keeping up. He did not like to make everyone wait for him. One morning he left the tent, telling the rest he was just going out for a while. But he never came back.

Only three men were left. Then a very bad blizzard came down and they were trapped in the tent. They had to sit and wait for the storm to stop. But it went on for so long that they ran out of food and then out of fuel. They were starving and freezing. It was the end.

Next spring, some of the rest of the party went to look for them. They found the three men still in the tent. They had written letters about the trek and what had happened to them.

At present, the continent of Antarctica is protected. There is a base there, where researchers from all different lands can go to help study the Antarctic. It is called the Scott-Amundsen base.

What's in the book?

What continent is the South Pole in?

Did Scott reach the South Pole on his first expedition?

Why can the Antarctic only be explored in the summer?

What do you think?

Was Scott a hero or a failure?

Why did the three men write letters before they died?

Underground

The ground under our feet seems solid and hard, but in fact there are lots of things under it.

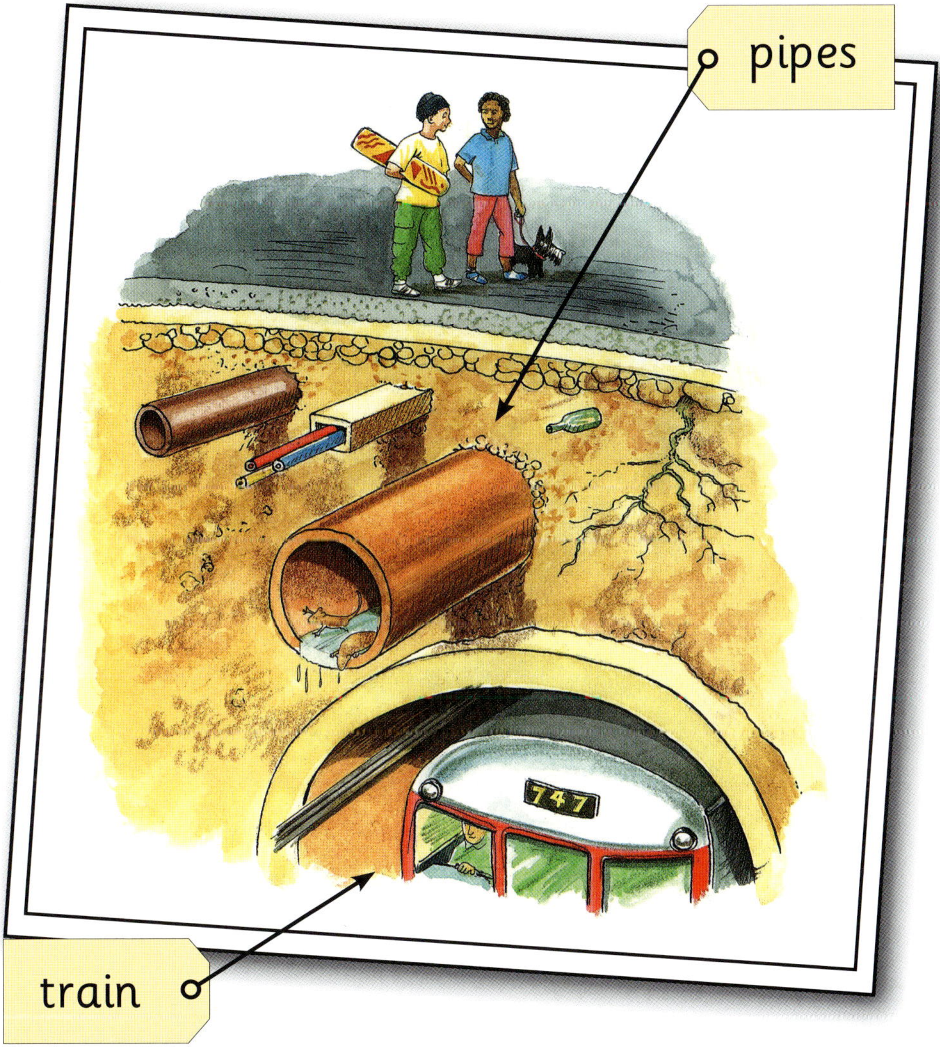

We live on a planet called Earth, which was formed a long time ago. The Earth is round in shape, like a ball. It is covered by a thin crust of rock.

Rock is made up of things called minerals. This is one sort of rock, called granite. You can see the different minerals in the granite.

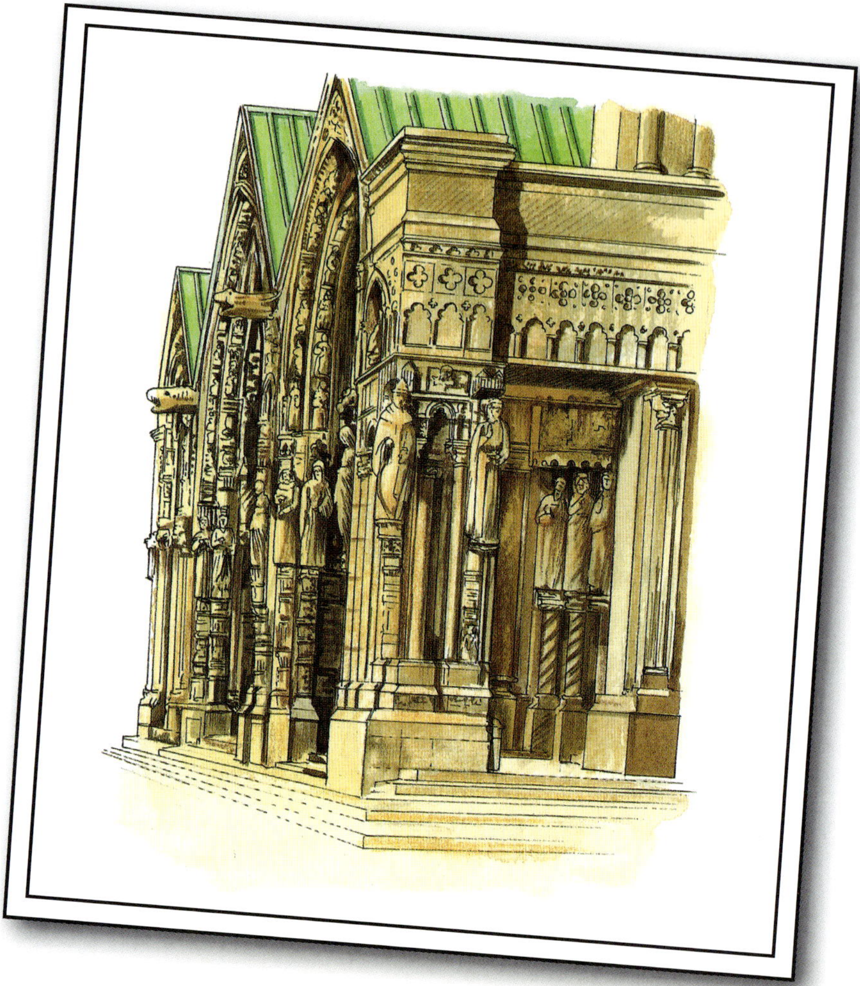

This building is made from a sort of rock called limestone. Limestone is good for building things as it is strong and can be carved into shapes.

Where limestone is found, there are often underground caves and holes. These are made by rain. Little by little, the rain digs caves and tunnels into the rock.

As the rain drips, it mixes with some of the minerals from the limestone and together they form columns in the caves. The columns that hang down are called stalactites and those that stick up are called stalagmites.

Explorers investigate underground caves and tunnels. They need hard hats, torches and sometimes ropes.

Oil and gas are found under the ground. A long time ago, very small animals died and bit by bit they sank deep down into the earth. Little by little, mud and sand collected on top of them. When the animals' remains had been mixed with the mud and sand for a long time, they ended up forming oil and gas.

Coal can be found under the ground too. Coal is what is left from trees that died and rotted a long time ago. We dig down into the ground to get the coal out. The hole we dig to do this is called a mine.

Tunnels with roads and tracks are built under the ground for cars and trains to travel along. Some of these tunnels go under rivers and some go from country to country.

Much of the rock that covers the Earth is topped with a thin coating of soil. Some animals can dig down into the soil and make homes underground. Where there is no soil, the land is just a rocky desert.

rabbits

foxes

wombats

moles

ants

groundhogs

Tree roots go down into the ground too. The roots keep the trees steady and stop them from falling down. Trees use roots to take in food from the soil as well.

We get some of our food from under the ground.

carrots

radishes

beetroots

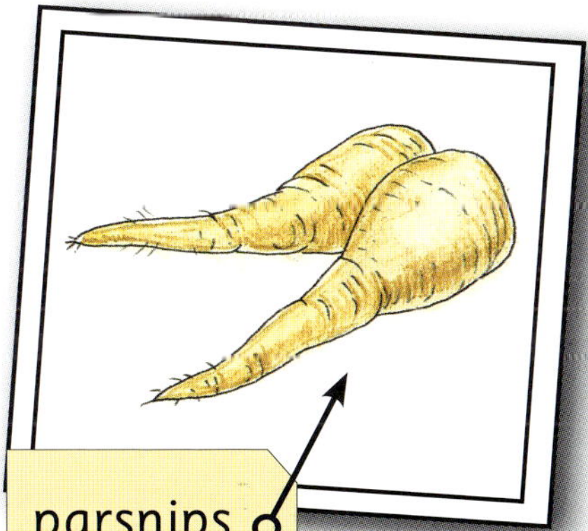

parsnips

yams

These are called root crops.

A long time ago, animals like these used to live on the Earth.

The bones, teeth and eggs of these animals have been found in some very old rocks. Sometimes you can just see the shape where they used to be in the rock. Rocks like these are called fossils.

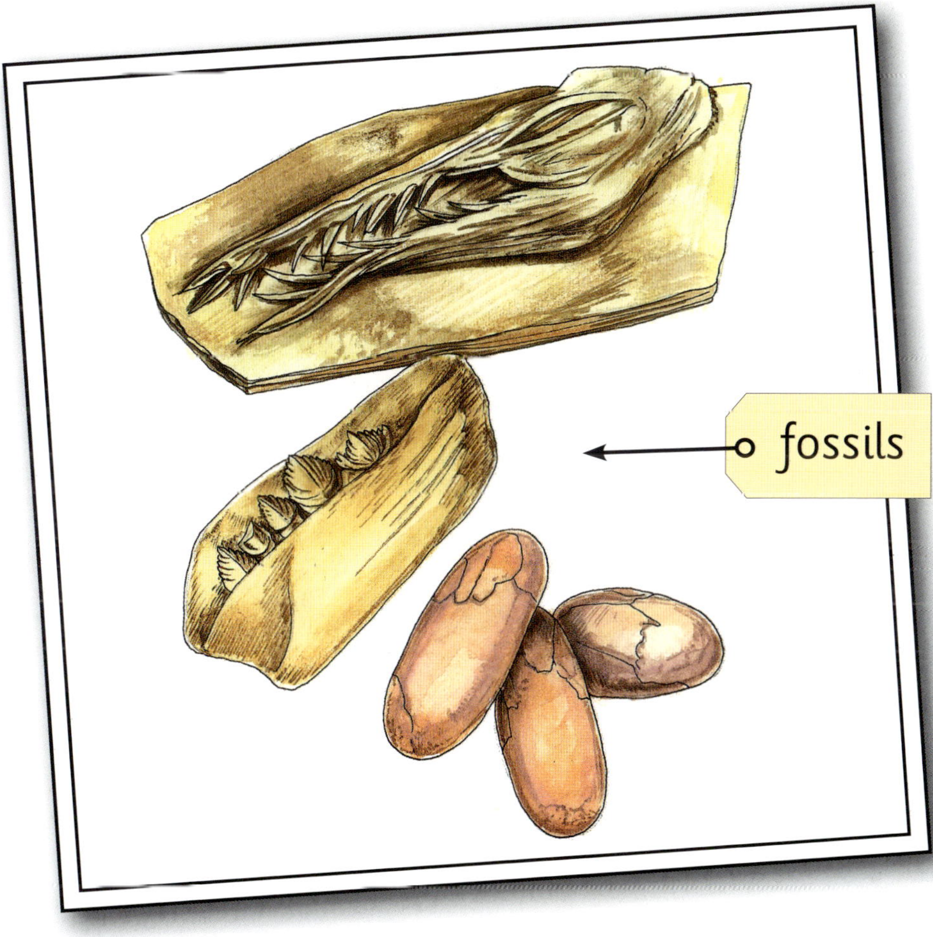

Under the ground are all sorts of things that have been left from times gone by. There are coins, bits of pottery and sometimes old houses! When they are found, they can be dug up and used to help us understand what life was like back then.

So next time you look down, think about all the things that are found under the ground.

What's in the book?

What is limestone good for?

What are stalactites and stalagmites?

What animals live under the ground?

What do you think?

Why do underground explorers wear hard hats?

Why do we dig up coal from the ground?

Mushrooms

Mushrooms and toadstools are a sort of fungus. Some are edible, but some are poisonous. It is very difficult to tell them apart.

Mushrooms and toadstools have a stem that comes up from the ground with a cap on top. Under the cap, there are lines running out from the middle. These lines are called gills.

On the gills are spores. Spores are the seeds of mushrooms and toadstools. There are thousands of spores on the gills of a mushroom.

The spores travel on the wind. When they land, they develop small white threads. Mushrooms or toadstools develop from these threads.

Mushrooms and toadstools do not have roots. Instead the small white threads spread out from the stem under the ground. The stem is made up of these threads.

Mushrooms are often found in rings. The threads under the ground travel out and so the ring gets a bit bigger. The threads and mushrooms in the middle of the ring die.

Mushrooms and toadstools start out looking like small buttons. The gills under the cap cannot be seen as the skin on the top is attached to the stem. As the mushroom or toadstool gets bigger, the skin stretches until it rips. You can see the ring of skin on the stem where it was attached.

Mushrooms and toadstools use the threads under the ground to get food. A liquid seeps out of the threads and into the soil, or wood, where the mushroom is. This liquid makes the dead stuff in the soil, or wood, liquid too. The threads then take in all this liquid as food, and it travels up the stem to the rest of the mushroom or toadstool.

Mushrooms and toadstools are found in woods, on trees, in dark damp spots, as well as in gardens.

The deathcap toadstool is very poisonous. It has a little cup at the bottom of the stem. It starts with a pointed white cap, but as it gets bigger, the cap gets flatter and darker. It has a sweet, sickly smell.

Bracket fungus is found on trees. It rots the wood of the tree. Bracket fungus can get very big. Some live on dead wood, but some attack living trees.

These mushrooms are shaggy inkcaps. The cap twists up and a dark liquid drips to the ground. They are often seen on the side of roads or on rubbish dumps.

Puffballs are round, white mushrooms. They can get as big as footballs. When they are ripe, they explode and a cloud of spores puffs out.

This is a stinkhorn. It starts as a small, white ball. When it gets bigger, it has a dark cap. The cap is very smelly. This smell attracts flies.

The fungus called dead man's fingers is found on tree stumps. It is black on the outside but white on the inside. It has a short, twisted stem which gets bigger at the top so they look a bit like fingers, which is where it gets its name from.

Truffles are a sort of fungus that develop under the ground. Truffles are used in cooking and are very expensive. Pigs can smell truffles. Farmers train pigs to root out the truffles.

What's in the book?

What are spores?
What do mushrooms
and toadstools have instead of roots?
Where do mushrooms and
toadstools grow?

What do you think?

Why shouldn't you pick mushrooms
and eat them?
Are mushrooms you buy in food shops
safe to eat?

Teeth

Smile! What do you see? A mouth, lips and teeth. Teeth help us to bite into our food and cut it up into smaller lumps.

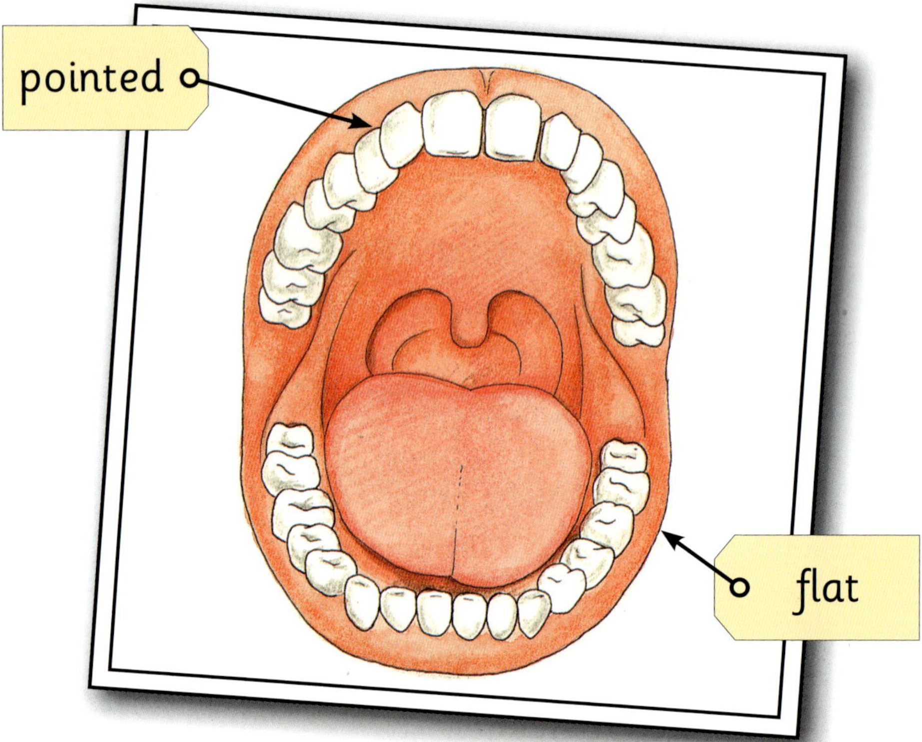

Different shaped teeth have different jobs. Some are shaped like spades and we use them to bite into food. Some are sharp and pointed, so as to shred the lumps of food into smaller bits. Then there are wide, flat teeth at the back of the mouth, which mash the food into a pulp.

When we are born, we have no teeth that can be seen yet. The teeth are all hidden under our gums. When they start to develop, they can make the gums sore. This is called teething.

We have more than one set of teeth. As small children, we get a set of milk teeth. There are only twenty of these milk teeth. They start to wobble and fall out when we are about six or seven.

Then we get our next set of teeth. These adult teeth are much bigger and are all we get for the rest of our lives. So it is very important to keep them healthy.

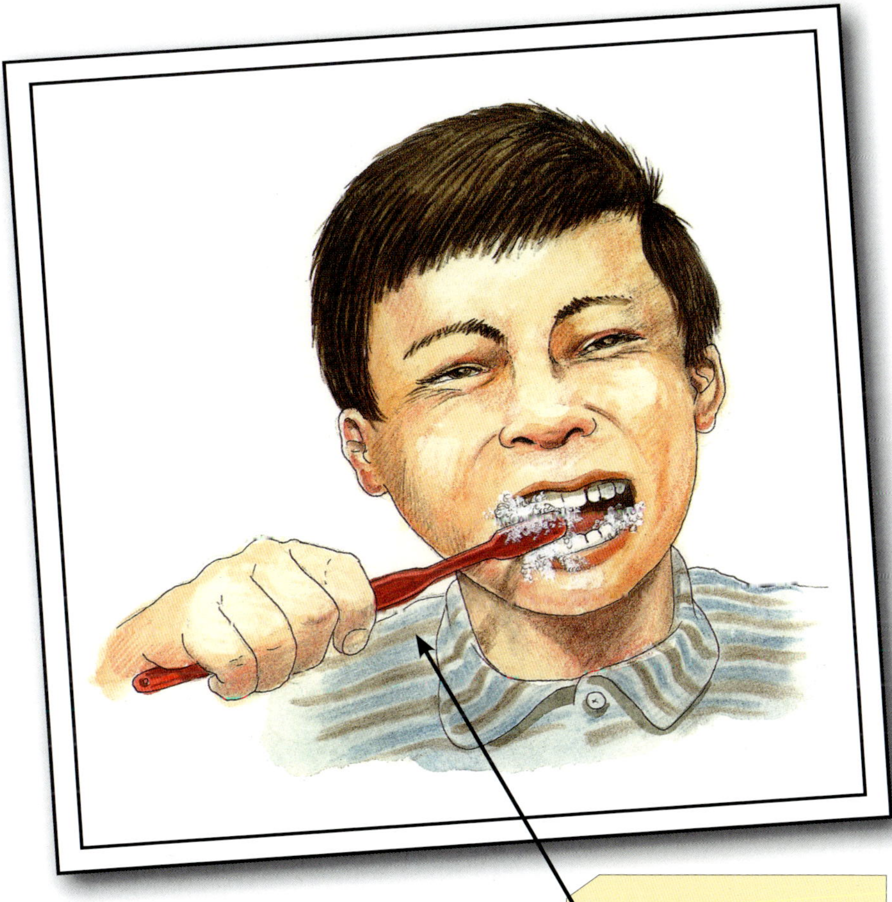

Inside the mouth, it is dark and wet. There are some living things so small that we cannot see them. They like dark and wetness, so they live and breed inside our mouths.

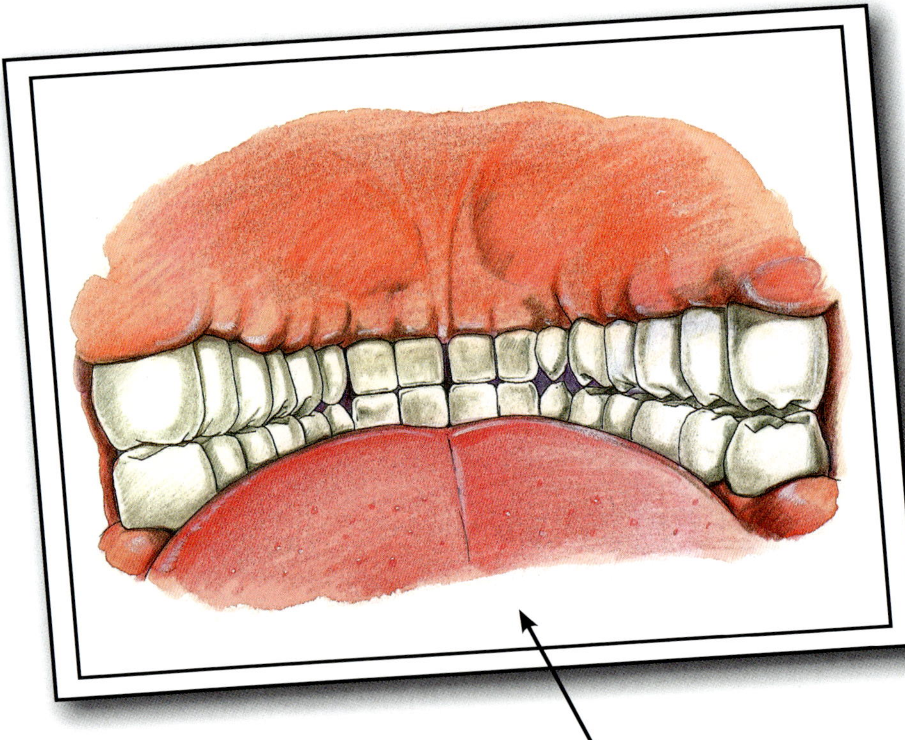

inside the mouth

If they breed on food which has stuck to our teeth, the teeth can rot and go bad.

Brushing our teeth can help stop this happening. This is why teeth need to be brushed when you get up in the morning and before you go to bed. Brush the inside, outside and top of the teeth.

Some food is good for teeth.

Some food is bad for teeth.

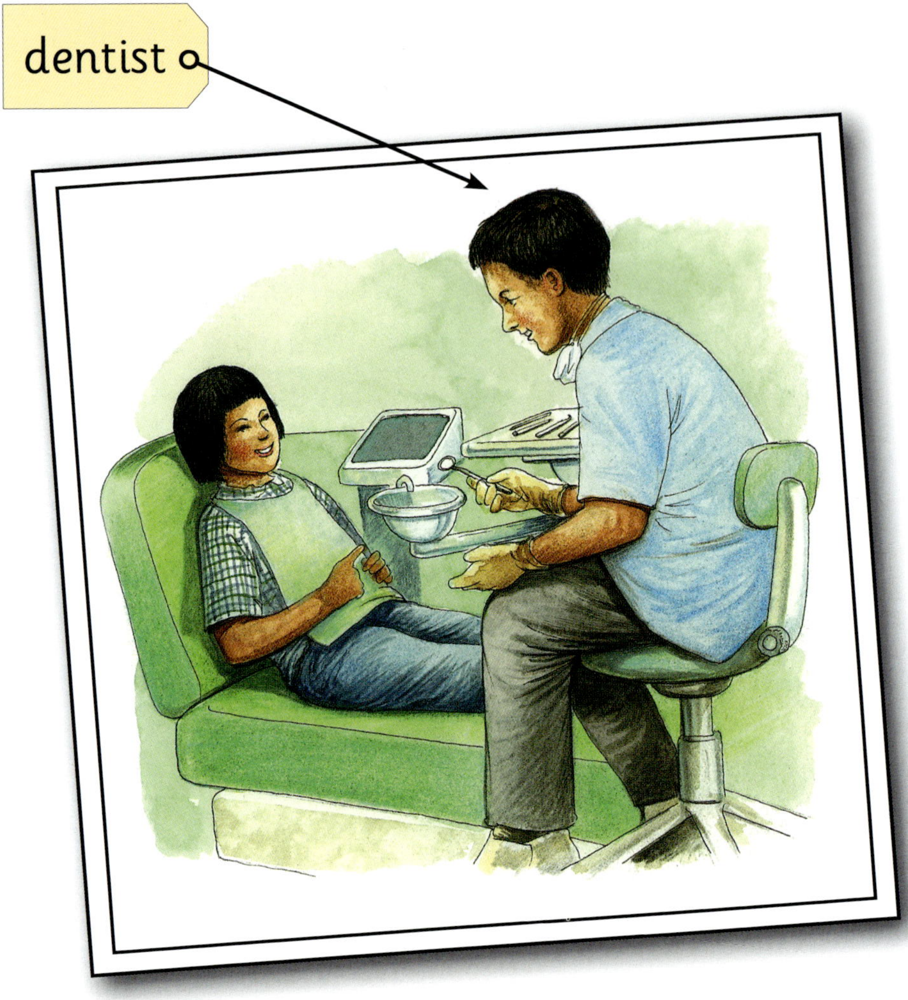

Dentists are trained to help us protect our teeth and gums. They have lots of different equipment.

Dentists have a lamp, which they shine into the mouth so they can see it better. Then they use a small mirror to help them see all the teeth. They poke around with a sort of metal toothpick, which helps them look for holes.

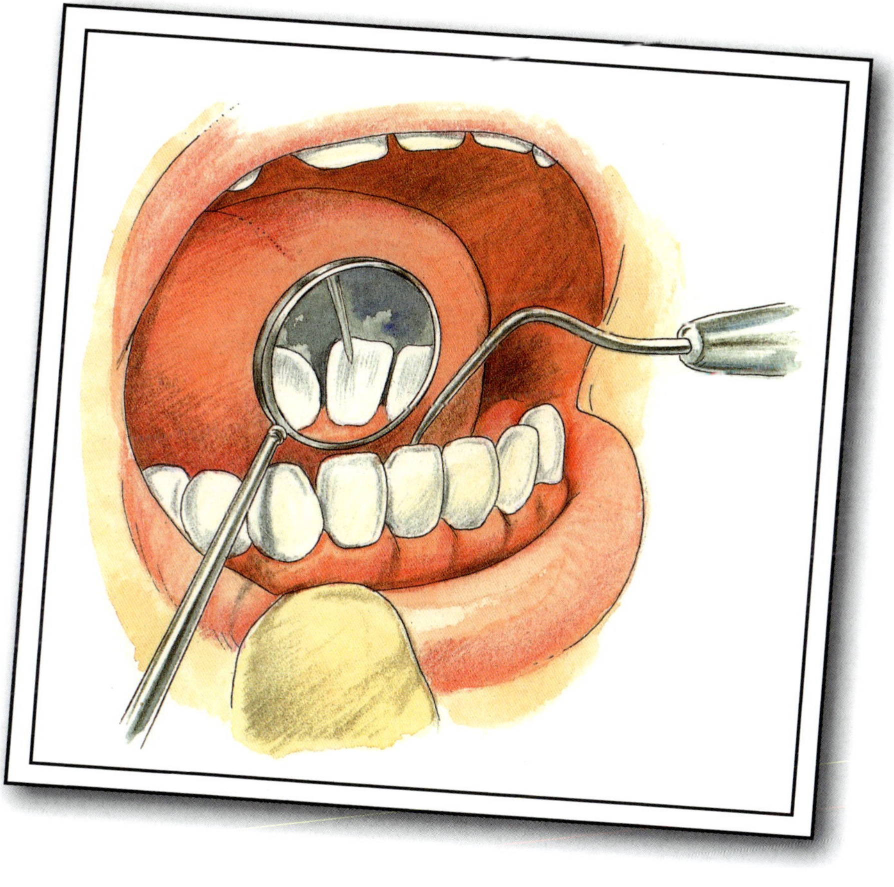

If a tooth has a hole in it, it needs a filling to stop the rot spreading. The dentist starts by injecting a painkiller into the gum to make it numb. Then the dentist drills out the rotten part of the tooth. The hole that is left is called a cavity, and this is what the dentist fills.

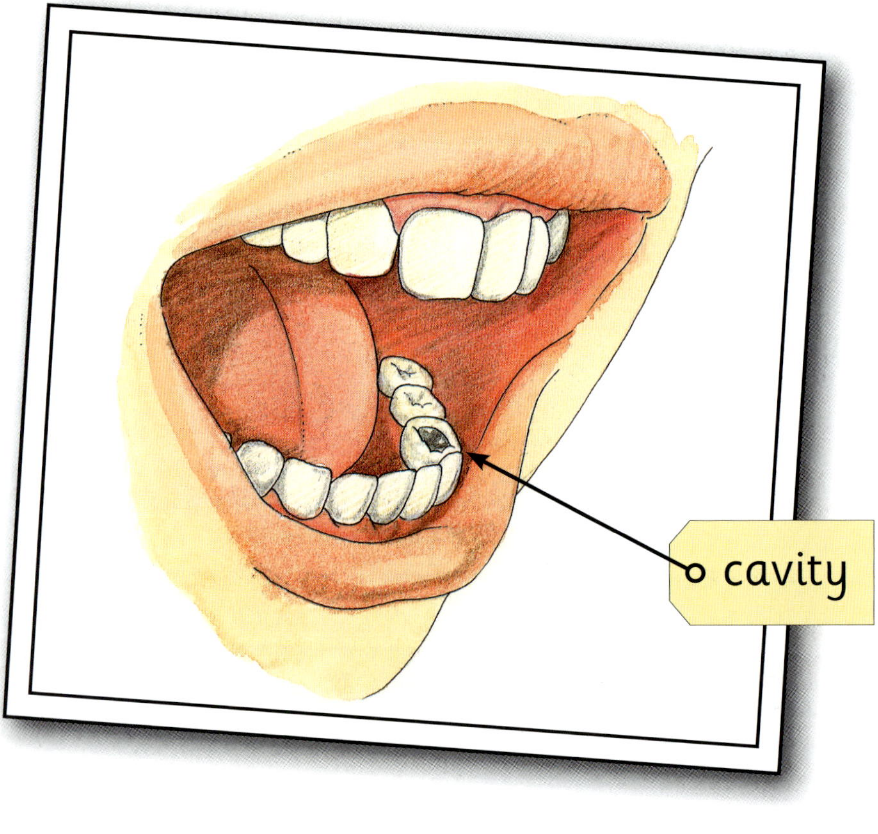

A tooth is made up of three main parts. It has a root, which joins it to the gum and to the rest of the skull. Then, on the inside, there are lots of nerves. It is the nerves which sometimes feel pain. The outside of the tooth is coated with white enamel, which is very hard.

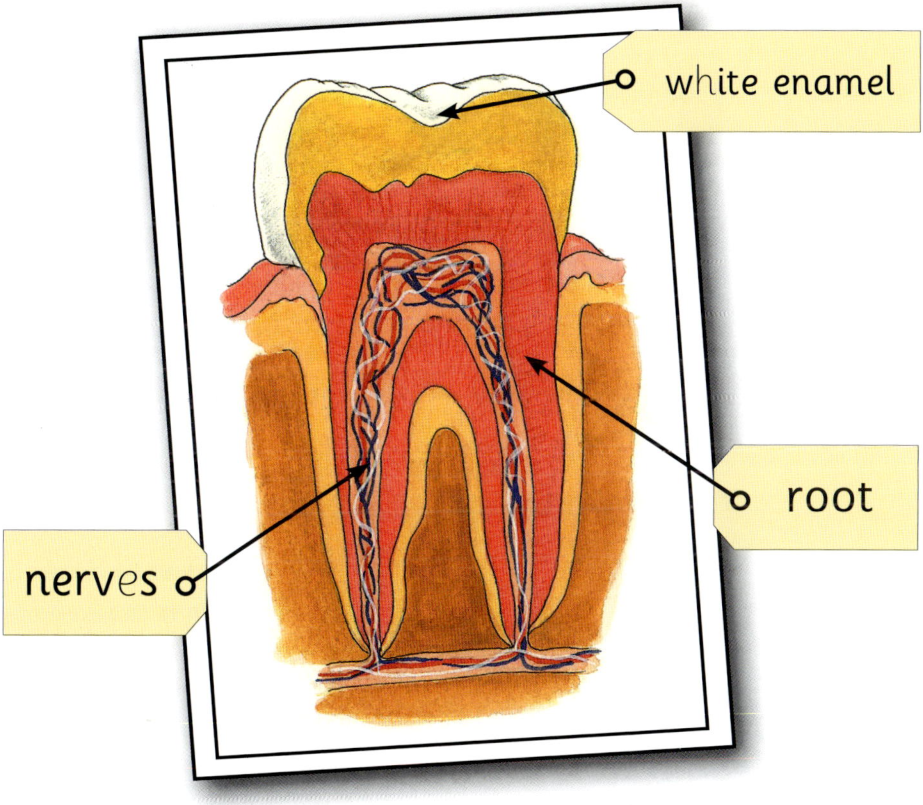

Different animals have different sorts of teeth. Animals' teeth have adapted to do all sorts of different jobs. Tusks are the biggest sort of teeth.

Animals such as rabbits, squirrels, lemmings and muskrats have long, strong teeth. These teeth keep on getting bigger and must be used often or they will get too long. Pet rabbits sometimes have to have long teeth filed down by a vet if they have not nibbled much hard food.

Sharks have very sharp, pointed teeth. They develop teeth all the time. So if one tooth drops or falls out, they have a second one waiting to fill the gap. So sharks never run out of teeth!

What's in the book?

Why are teeth
different shapes?
How many milk teeth do humans have?
What do dentists do?

What do you think?

Why do you need to brush your teeth
in the morning?
How often should you visit the dentist?

Parents

An important part of becoming a confident, fluent reader is a child's ability to understand what they are reading. Below are some suggestions on how to develop a child's reading comprehension.

Make reading this book a shared experience between you and the child. Try to avoid leaving it until the whole book is read before talking about it. Occasionally stop at various intervals throughout the book.

Ask questions about the characters, the setting, the action and the meaning.

Encourage the child to think about what might happen next. It does not matter if the answer is right or wrong, so long as the suggestion makes sense and demonstrates understanding.

Ask the child to describe what is happening in the illustrations.

Relate what is happening in the book to any real-life experiences the child may have.

Pick out any vocabulary that may be new to the child and ask what they think it means. If they don't know, explain it and relate it to what is happening in the book.

Encourage the child to summarise, in their own words, what they have read.

Book Review

Try to answer these questions about each book in this compilation:

What was the book about and what was the book trying to do?

Did you learn anything from reading this book?

What was your favourite fact in this book? Why did you like it?

Were you surprised by any of the facts in this book?

Did you like the illustrations? Why?

Are you interested to learn more about the topic in this book?

Do you think anyone you know would enjoy this book?

Could you talk about this book in your own words?

Have you heard anything about the topic in this book before?

Would you have liked this book to be shorter or longer?

Were there any parts of the book that you didn't like?

Have you read any books that are similar to this one?

Would you enjoy reading this book again and would you recommend it to a friend?

Topic Review

Choose a topic in this book to think about:

What is the topic?

Why is it interesting to you?

Describe what you have learned about it.

Why is this topic important to you?

Has reading about this topic inspired you to do anything?

What other things would you like to know about this topic?